Arrivals

Jeremy Abrahams

Distributed by Jeremy Abrahams
info@jeremyabrahams.co.uk
www.jeremyabrahams.co.uk

Designed by Tom Howey
www.tomhowey.com

Printed and published by:
Northend Creative Print Solutions
Clyde Rd, Sheffield S8 0TZ

ISBN: 978-0-9935393-0-5

Arrivals
Making Sheffield Home
Jeremy Abrahams

For arrivals everywhere

Foreword

The Arrivals project encompasses many issues that are close to my heart. In 1939, as an 11 year old refugee, I came to the UK from Prague on the Kindertransport. Jews in Prague were well aware of the danger they were in, having had first hand information from families fleeing from persecution in Germany and Austria. The rest of the world had closed its doors to these refugees, apart from Britain, which agreed under certain conditions to accept children – and so the Kindertransport came into being. My Jewish parents took the brave decision to send me on such a transport at the end of June 1939. What they thought would be a temporary measure became a life changing event.

For years I have used this experience to try to convey to both children and adults how hatred of others can have devastating consequences for individuals, families, communities and even countries. I have also tried to show how, at the same time, such consequences can bring out the best in people - the

Kindertransport saved the lives of 10,000 children. Sheffield has been my home since 1939, and I am proud to live in the place which, in 2007, became the UK's first 'City of Sanctuary' for asylum-seekers and refugees.

Jeremy's images show us our shared humanity and bring a positive message about migration, which I hope will resonate with a wide audience both in Sheffield and beyond. His book comes at a time when migration issues are high on our political agenda; it tells the stories of people who have found a welcome in Sheffield, and who have contributed to and enriched this city. Some of his subjects have come, like me, as a refugee. Others have come by invitation from Commonwealth countries and former British colonies. And many have taken up their right to live and work here as EU citizens. Their images and stories stand as portraits of 72 individuals; but taken together they are a joyous and uplifting portrait of a creative and diverse city.

Sue Pearson

Introduction

Migration is one of the pre-eminent issues of our age. The flow of people fleeing war and persecution and the free movement of labour within the EU have made us all far more aware of immigration issues. And yet migration has always been with us; what seems to change most are our attitudes towards it. I wanted to remove immigration from the zone of contention and represent it positively, to humanise it through the images and stories of the people who have migrated from around the world to Sheffield. Immigration is often portrayed as a homogenous process. In reality there isn't one reason for immigration, there aren't even several reasons – there are countless reasons, as many reasons as there are people.

When I was a teacher I met Sue Pearson, who came to Sheffield from Prague on the Kindertransport in 1939 as an 11 year old girl and never saw her parents again. She was adopted by a Sheffield family and grew up to become a nursery school headteacher and to foster many children in addition to her own. In retirement Sue started visiting schools, talking about the Kindertransport and drawing parallels between events in the 1930s and today.

When Sue spoke to my classes her ability to utilise the natural empathy that children felt for her to affect their attitudes to current migrants inspired my teaching and sowed a seed that became 'Arrivals'.

When my education career ended in 2013 I fulfilled a lifetime ambition and trained as a professional photographer. What began life as a student project at Sheffield College lasted three years and grew into 'Arrivals'. At the time, what is now an ongoing campaign against migrants in much of the media had just begun, and I wanted to counteract that in my own small way. I wanted to visually represent the idea that immigration has always been with us and to share the images and stories of people who have migrated from overseas to Sheffield. By photographing one person who arrived from overseas in each year from 1945 to 2016 I created portraits of seventy two people and a portrait of the pattern of migration. And by asking each person where in Sheffield they wanted their picture taken I showed that they had indeed become part of our community and had made Sheffield their home.

Pierre Ngunda Kabaya is a refugee from the Democratic Republic of the Congo. When I asked him whether there was somewhere special in Sheffield where I should take his picture, he told me that anywhere would be fine as all of Sheffield was beautiful. Many people had spoken of their love of Sheffield as a green city, but I was still a little surprised by Pierre's perspective, so I asked if he was sure. He told me again that it was all beautiful and got out his phone to show me a picture of the refugee camp he lived in for seven years. 'Believe me', he said, 'it's all beautiful'. So I took him to the roof of the University of Sheffield's Arts Tower, where he could see all of his beautiful new home.

When I met Tanya Schmoller, she told me that she had worked for Allen Lane, the founder of Penguin Books, for many years, but that she mainly dealt with correspondence. I only discovered later that this correspondence importantly included dealing with the Lady Chatterley's Lover obscenity trial, which ended in triumph for Penguin Books and freedom of expression.

Some pictures, like that of Pedro Fuentes at Sheffield Forgemasters, tell their own story - that Sheffield, the steel city, has always relied on migrant labour. Others need more information to help us understand their full significance. Haji Dodola and three of his children photographed in the Peace Gardens looks like a simple snapshot of a family spending some time in one of Sheffield's favourite locations. However, when we learn that two of the children were born in a refugee camp where 'snakes, scorpions and malaria were an ever present danger', its significance changes.

Many of the people I have photographed have spoken so positively of the warmth of the reception they have received here. It's a cliché that people make places, but it is true. As Magali Fleurot put it, 'come and spend time here and you too will feel part of it'. That welcome was also extended to me as the photographer; so many iconic Sheffield locations opened their doors to me and gave me free rein, such as Sheffield City Hall and Sheffield Cathedral, where I photographed Rawan Dardok and Ahmed Maani just before Christmas 2015.

'Arrivals: Making Sheffield Home' is about migration, it's about people and it's about Sheffield. Sheffield is a unique city; but its experiences are shared by countless cities around the world.

Jeremy Abrahams
Sheffield, 2016

Tanya Schmoller

I've no idea why my father was in Uruguay. He told me he had had to leave Russia for good, but I didn't have the sense to ask him why. Still, I'm the only person in the country to have been at the World Cup final in Montevideo in 1930!

My mother was English so English was spoken at home. In 1945 I was working for the British Council when Allen Lane (the founder of Penguin Books) arrived. He asked what my ambitions were. I wanted to go to the London School of Economics, so he offered me a job at Penguin which meant I could go to night school. Flying was the only means of travel, but as an ordinary passenger, I got off-loaded at every stop, and it took me 3 months to get to England, staying in exciting places such as Lima and New York.

At Penguin I mainly ensured Allen Lane attended to correspondence; I also met my husband Hans there. He had left Berlin in 1937 by getting a job at a printing works in Basutoland (now Lesotho), which had advertised for a Christian, but got a Jew.

Tanya died peacefully on 14 January 2016, six weeks before her 98th birthday, with her family around her.

‹ At home in Nether Edge

< Moore Street Roundabout, Inner Ring Road

2000
Keitumetsi Motlogwa

I came from Zimbabwe to study nursing, where I found a friendly welcoming community, a thriving cycling scene, an exciting music hub and ended up as an electrician. For a slice of home I've spent the last few years as part of Sounds of Southern Africa, a musical project that aims to be an educational and cultural exchange that links schools and the general public in Yorkshire and Bulawayo.

1965

George Grant

I'm the youngest of ten children. My Dad came to Sheffield from Jamaica in 1960 and I came with my Mum and five other siblings in 1965.

I spent a lot of time in Meersbrook Park, playing football and getting into mischief. Sheffield United wanted to sign me as a schoolboy, but I didn't fancy all the training. I've expended just as much energy working as a self employed builder!

Meersbrook Park >

2012
Haji
Dodola

As an Oromo child in Ethiopia I looked after goats and sheep, but I studied chemistry at Addis Ababa University. After the corrupt 2005 election students protested; I was arrested and my studies were halted.

I left for Kenya and spent 6 years in a refugee camp where I worked for the UN as a lab assistant, met my wife and our two oldest children were born. My aim is to retrain as a lab assistant and work in a local hospital.

‹ Peace Gardens

2013

Francisco Requena-Silvante

In 2013 unemployment in Spain reached 26 percent. Ana lost her job as an accountant and I had no chance of progression in my academic career. We considered the possibility to migrate to the UK where Ana and I met, married and lived between 1994 and 2001. I got a job as Reader in Economics at the University of Sheffield and shortly after Ana started working for Sheffield Forgemasters.

Ecclesall Woods >

1991

Maya Moudnani

I left home in Morocco at 16 and worked as a volunteer in various Western African countries, some at war, some not.

Wanting a break from war's devastation, I accepted an invitation from the British Consulate to teach in Northern Ireland but then came to Cambridge, from where I followed love all the way to Sheffield!

I can't imagine living anywhere else but in Sheffield, great city of sanctuary.

‹ 'Angry Woman' sculpture by George Fullard, Upper Chapel forecourt

Butcher Works, City Centre ›

1971

Marion Tylecote

As a Fine Art student in Durban, South Africa, I was involved in opposing the apartheid regime. As it became difficult to live with being an opponent of the system, I decided to move to Britain, the land of my ancestors. In Sheffield, I joined a group opposed to apartheid and deeply appreciated my new freedoms.

2007

Chaithra Chinnaraj

I came from Bangalore in southern India, arriving in Sheffield on a pleasant sunny day in June 2007. It's been my home ever since. Lots of things have changed since then, new building and new developments, but the people remain warm and friendly, which is one of the things I love most about Sheffield.

The city has taught me a great deal. I was married as a very young girl, but it is here that I have learnt about life and grown into a confident young woman. In my time here we have faced a lot of ups and downs, but Sheffield has kept us positive. It has been the most amazing roller coaster ride.

Sheffield is truly a jewel set in a stunning crown of green. I am looking forward to the rest of my life here and the experiences it will bring.

Wanlin Steele

I trained as a dancer in China at the Beijing Dance Academy. After graduation I became a dancer, teacher and choreographer. I toured China and performed on national television.

In Sheffield with my husband David most of my time was spent with our two sons. I'd always wanted to share Chinese dance with Sheffield and so Wanlin Dance School was born.

‹ Sheffield University Drama Studios

Sharrowvale Road ›

1990
Lee Choo

I was raised the daughter of hard working Chinese parents who ran a watch repair shop near Kuala Lumpur. An English convent education in this former British colony led me to London to study optometry.

My thriving optometry practice on Sharrow Vale has provided me with a rewarding life and the cooler climate makes my outdoor activities - cycling and tennis - more enjoyable.

Pierre Ngunda Kabaya

In May 2004 I called MONUSCO, the United Nations Mission in the Democratic Republic of the Congo, and they escorted me over the border to Rwanda. My brother had been killed by the government in a conflict with rebels in our region of South Kivu, and I was scared that I would be next. I spent three months in a transit camp then seven years in Kibwye refugee camp, where I met my wife. In October 2010 the UK Border Agency came to the camp and selected 72 out of 20,000 people to come to the UK. In January 2011 we arrived in the UK and were helped to resettle by the Refugee Council's Gateway programme.

In the Congo and the camp I didn't know my future - will I live for tomorrow? Here in the UK I feel free, I can sleep easy and my children go to school. Soon I will be a British citizen and I will be able to get a student loan and return to University. I had the grace to come from the refugee camp to England and I must grasp the opportunity.

Roof of the Arts Tower, University of Sheffield >

Malaka Mohammed Shwaikh

< University of Sheffield Students' Union

I was given a fee waiver to study for a Masters in Global Politics and Law at the University of Sheffield. Travelling here from Gaza/Palestine was not easy. I had a UK visa and plane tickets but I could not travel. I kept trying and finally made it, despite experiencing humiliation and discrimination many times when I tried to cross the border from Gaza. I finally arrived here feeling traumatised. It took some time to start engaging with the community around me. Since those early days I have spoken throughout Europe about the situation in Palestine and Yaffa, my homeland.

Studying in Sheffield has helped me to address the international community effectively. In 2014 I was elected the Students' Union education officer with the highest number of votes in the history of the Students' Union.

1994

Adam
Funk

I came to the UK from the USA when I got married. I've always enjoyed the parks, Henderson's Relish, the libraries and museums, and the ethnic grocery stores. I've come to enjoy cricket, although I don't appreciate football.

It seems strange to me that people sometimes talk the city down – they say things like 'Why would you want to live here?' I guess they don't notice all the things I appreciate here.

‹ Sheffield Cathedral

General Cemetery >

1988

Gabrielle Vajra

I arrived to spend a year as a French assistant in two Rotherham schools. When the train finally stopped in Sheffield the culture shock couldn't have been bigger, but the more I saw the more I liked it. It was big, green and friendly and I immediately felt at home. I had no idea I would settle and have a family here, but now I wouldn't have it any other way.

Seiko Kinoshita

After my BA, I worked as a textile designer and computer aided design operator in Japan, but I always wanted to be an artist. A scholarship from the Japanese Rotary Club enabled me to do an MA in Textile Design at Nottingham Trent University, along with help from my Rotarian host in Derby.

I chose to come to the UK because I particularly liked the works of British textile artists. On completing my MA I applied for, and was selected for, the Starter Studio Programme at Yorkshire Artspace, Sheffield. I have had my studio at Yorkshire Artspace ever since and have had many art commissions including the 'Blue Bird' installation at Sheffield Central Library.

Persistence Works, Yorkshire Artspace >

Peter Butler

I was born in Dublin, but only lived there until I was five. My father's new job caused us to move. It was a very cold December day when I first saw Sheffield. There was no central heating in the house we had rented, but the landlord had assured my father that coal fires would be lit for us. After a long journey, our family of 5 arrived to find that this had not been done. My father had some harsh things to say to the landlord when he arrived on the scene.

The most exciting discovery in our new neighbourhood was Millhouses Park and the boating pond was my favourite spot. Small paddle boats, which were easy for children to use, could be hired. Adults would put remote control boats in the water, which we had to avoid. But one day I 'accidentally' sank one of these boats. Perhaps that's why they won't let me on the boats anymore!

‹ Millhouses Park

2003

Souleymane Bah

After escaping political persecution in Guinea I sought asylum in the UK. Throughout the long and difficult period before I was granted leave to remain I liked to sit next to the bamboo in the Winter Garden and think about my Grandma. I had always helped her cut bamboo to repair her house. City workers helped me think positively about my future and gave me the ambition to have an education. Sheffield is now my home for life.

< Winter Garden

At home in Broomhill ›

1992

Eva Kaltenthaler

I am from the USA and met my English husband in Malawi, where I worked as a public health volunteer. We came to Sheffield with our two young daughters in 1992 and then also had twin daughters.

I am a Professor in the School of Health and Related Research at the University of Sheffield. Sheffield is a warm and friendly city and I have always felt welcome. It feels like home now. I can't imagine living anywhere else.

1948

Marina Lewycka

My parents came from Ukraine. It was a troubled country at a troubled time. By the age of 35 my mother had lived through World War I, the Russian Revolution, the Civil War, two famines, the execution of her father under Stalin, World War II, and deportation into forced labour camps in Germany, where they survived aerial Allied bombing. I was born in a Displaced Persons' camp in Schleswig Holstein in 1946.

I have no memories of that early time, but I have got one or two photographs. As I grew up, I can remember that we were treated with great kindness, and a bit of leg-pulling, by our wonderful Yorkshire neighbours, who never once made us feel unwelcome here. I moved to Sheffield in 1985 with my husband, who worked at the National Union of Mineworkers and it has been my home ever since.

Jan Kot/
Danuta Reah

My father, Jan Kot, was born in Baranovichi in western Belarus. He studied engineering at Warsaw University, but at the start of WWII, joined the Polish cavalry and fought Stalin's invading Red Army. He was taken prisoner but escaped, crossing Europe and coming to the UK to join the Polish Free Forces where he became a paratrooper. Having opposed Stalin, he was not able to return to Poland after the war. He studied at the Polish School of Architecture at Liverpool University where he trained as an architect, and met his future wife, Margaret Woodcock. He came to Sheffield in 1949 to join the City Architect's Department. He eventually became City Architect, and was responsible for many school and college buildings, most notably the Wedding Cake registry office, and the 'egg box' Town Hall extension, both sadly lost to redevelopment. He loved his adopted country, but always remained a Pole at heart.

‹ On the site of former Town Hall extension

Dale Le Fevre

I was living in the Californian woods in my dream house. My wife, who was from Sheffield, wanted to return. I was devastated. Being self-employed teaching cooperative New Games, it's hard to establish in a new place. But I crossed the pond.

We split up a year later, but I made friends and liked living in Sheffield with its cultural advantages, such as SOSA XA!, the Southern African choir I sing in.

‹ Whiteley Woods

Madina Mosque >

1979
Mohammed Amin

Both of my grandfathers and my father were in the British Army. After independence I was in the Pakistan Army. My uncle had come to Sheffield with his family after independence and when I left the Pakistan Army I came to visit. A marriage was arranged for me here and so I settled in Sheffield, falling in love and bringing up two children.

Tony Brock

I came to this country from Dublin at just 25 years of age having met and married a young lady from Stocksbridge. My first job was at Sammy Fox's Steelworks in their melting shop. I will never forget the shock of walking in there and seeing for the first time the flying sparks and molten steel being poured out of the furnace! Even the floor was scorching hot so exchanging my shoes for clogs was a necessity as was the thick woollen shirt which regularly became stuck to my back at the end of each shift. It was all a dramatic change from being a happy little postman cycling around in the fresh air in Dublin, the city by the sea!

My workmates took some time to accept me and of course I became known as Paddy from the start. For quite a while they seemed to resent my presence as they objected to 'foreigners' coming and marrying 'their girls'!

Eventually I moved to Sheffield with my wife and four children having obtained a staff job as a quality inspector with the British Steel Corporation. A somewhat more congenial number!

Bolehills >

‹ Channing Hall

Tareq Al Khaleeli

Before the war I felt at peace in Iraq. Everything changed after the war; danger from bombs and snipers was everywhere, there was no work, everyone was tense and anxious. In 2006 my family left for Damascus in Syria. I first wrote to the United Nations High Commissioner for Refugees in 2007 to ask to if we could become refugees in a safe country. We waited nine years for something to happen. During this time the civil war started in Syria, my Iraqi passport expired and as a result I had to walk to the authorities every day for 6 months.

Finally, in 2015, I was interviewed online by British immigration officials and given a visa to come to the UK. The day before we were due to leave for England we were stopped at a checkpoint - but allowed to go when they saw our UK visas.

Now we are happy and at peace. My children go to school and we are all learning English. But I still think of my close friend who remains in Syria, even though his mother is very ill, and I am trying to get help to get them out.

‹ The Ponderosa, Crookesmoor

1962

Clinton McKoy

I came from Jamaica in 1962 to join my father. I attended church and joined the Boy Scouts. I was bullied and faced racism. I didn't recognise it as racism at the time; I just knew that I felt uncomfortable in the environment.

The first youth club for Caribbean young people was set up in Crookesmoor; it was a place of comfort and safety, where I could meet friends, socialise and be myself.

1988

Ahmed Shaheen

I was raised in a beautiful valley in Kashmir, but left to complete my education, graduating in Lahore, then completing a Business Diploma at the Sorbonne in Paris. On a visit to Sheffield I met my future wife.

I started my first business in Sheffield; a restaurant called Rose of Kashmir. I became Chairman of the Pakistan Muslim Centre and in 2000 took the role of finance coordinator for a £5m community project to rebuild the Madina Mosque.

Millhouses Park >

2016

Dyah Setyana Noor

Pond's Forge >

I came to Sheffield to study for a Master's degree at Sheffield Hallam University. It didn't take long for me to fall in love with this lovely city, especially the fresh air and scenery that surrounds it, although I struggled when talking to local people with a different accent to the English I've learned. I lived in Manchester first but I found Sheffield a more comfortable place to live. Despite the wave of hate crime following the Brexit referendum, I haven't experienced or seen racial discrimination first hand. People I meet are warm and welcoming.

During my summer break I worked for Learn For Life Enterprise, a charity which helps refugees and asylum seekers to settle here. The awful hardships refugees have to endure have taught me a valuable lesson in life.

Taking a Master's degree means a lot to me. As a single mother of three who is not young anymore, I believe it's never too late to learn something new. I want to show women in my country, Indonesia, that there's always a way to pursue their dreams and they can do anything they put their mind to.

1963

Naveed Khan

Before the partition of India and Pakistan my father served in the British Army. Taking up his right of residency, he came to Sheffield in 1959. In 1963 he decided to bring his family. Well, most of it. I was sent to a school for army officers' sons but I ran away, enabling us all to come! My first job was making bricks for the grand sum of £12 per week!

‹ Attercliffe Hilltop Cemetery

St Matthew's Carver Street >

1968
Joseph
Durham

I came to the UK from Malaysia with my parents following the outbreak of ethnic conflict. I completed my education and went on to a fulfilling career in psychiatric nursing.

Immigration has transformed and energised local faith communities and the visits of Pope John Paul II and Pope Benedict were recognition of this. Britain has totally altered since I first arrived, but its tolerance and respect for the individual and civil liberties endures.

‹ In her studio in Walkley

1983

Annie Anthony Mays

I was born in Singapore of South Indian parents. In 1983 I married a British citizen and emigrated to Sheffield. Initially, Sheffield seemed grey, grim and cold. I started to paint my wallpaper to cheer myself up and have never stopped painting.

I studied art in Singapore and run workshops for refugees, asylum seekers and immigrants to break down their barriers through painting, crafts and conversation in English.

1974

Sandra Potesta

When I was offered a lecturing post in Cambridge, we packed our stuff, got in our Fiat 500 and drove all the way from Rome to England. What an adventure!

In 1974 I was appointed Principal Lecturer in Modern Languages at Sheffield City Polytechnic. I found that, yes, Sheffield has seven hills, like Rome, but the similarities stop there! I found Sheffield a friendly place, with excellent schools and beautiful parks.

Sheffield Hallam University >

Thomas Hezekiah Goode

I was born in the village of St. Catherines in Jamaica in 1932. I was one of the early wave of West Indian immigrants chasing the dream of a better life. In the former colonies the British government were advertising heavily to attract migrants to work in the nationalised industries. I worked in the steel industry for many years. We were made welcome by some people but life could be difficult in those early years. There was plenty of work but quality accommodation was difficult to find. There were still signs in the windows of rented properties reading 'No dogs, Irish or Niggers'. British women who fell for our exotic charms faced as much prejudice as we did. My wife was spat on in the street for her acquaintance with me. But over the years as populations have integrated life has become easier.

I have been a businessman for over 30 years. In addition to being a landlord I have a successful trading business. I have enjoyed my life in England and achieved so much. I may have been born in the West Indies but Sheffield is my home.

‹ Outside his shop on Abbeydale Road

Mohammed Nasir Ahmed

My father fought for the British Army in the First World War, when he was injured and treated in London, and in Italy and Burma during the Second World War. He came to England by invitation in the early 1960s and I joined him later with my mother, brother and sister. When we landed at Heathrow the fog, snow and extreme cold were beyond my experience.

I started school but I couldn't speak any English. My dad was friendly with the local priest and I used to visit his house where his wife would teach me English. Later I went to King Ecgbert school and encountered mixed classes - another shock for me! I was good at many sports and represented Sheffield in cross-country. I left school with Allah's blessings with 12 'O' levels and progressed to University College London to become a telecoms engineer. Employed by BT, my life had come full circle as I worked in Sheffield, Saudi Arabia and Pakistan. Now I am retired and and voluntarily help out at my local mosque.

Madina Mosque >

1995

Sabine Vanacker & David Kelly

Two 'accidental emigrants': David from Ireland and Sabine from Belgium, who met as postgraduate students at Hull University. We settled in Sheffield, halfway between Ireland and Belgium and on the railway line to Hull, where Sabine now works as a University Lecturer. We love Sheffield, its friendliness, trees and parks. We reckon that Sheffield has worked its magic ... it appears we've actually emigrated!

< Sheffield Station, Platform 2

Millenium Square >

2013

Elena &
Steve Trust

I grew up in Turin, Italy. I met my Cornish husband
Steve when I got a job in Switzerland. When the Swiss
branch of the business closed we thought Steve would
be transferred to the US but at the last minute he was
relocated to Sheffield. We knew nothing about Sheffield
before we got here but everyone has been so helpful to
us - we really do love the people here.

1998

Magali Fleurot

I studied English and Modern Languages to understand the words of my favourite bands and ended up in Sheffield as part of my university studies. South Yorkshire was a wonderful shock to the system: the "You alright love?", "Ay up sweetheart", the amazing countryside, the freedom to be who you are without being judged and most importantly - the people. Nowhere else have I come across such welcoming and kind people. My bus journeys are always full of nattering, I never feel like I am bothering someone by asking for the time or smiling!

If you are lost, do not be surprised if people not only explain in great detail how to get to your destination but often they will offer you a lift!

People often ask me, why have you left France, the food, the climate, and the glamour for Sheffield? Well come and spend time here and you too will feel part of it.

Pedro Fuentes

I remember being six years old, at home in Valparaíso, Chile, reading 'Made in Sheffield' on my mother's cutlery. In my early-twenties, as die designer for a Santiago engineering company, I recommended special steel made by Firth Brown of Sheffield.

In my mid-twenties, as a political prisoner in one of Pinochet's concentration camps in the north of Chile, I received an envelope containing a visa to live in the UK! I later discovered that my sister and my future wife had risked their lives to get me the visa from the UK Embassy. Once in the UK I learned that the visa was also a result of pressure on the British government by the Chile Solidarity Campaign and the trade union movement.

My first job in Sheffield was as a 'slinger' at Firth Brown, attaching loads to cranes. I was later promoted to utility man which involved slinging, crane driving and managing special steel gas furnaces.

In my sixties I was a teacher and organiser of classes for refugees from all over the world.

I feel thankful for the solidarity and support I have received throughout my exile here and I am proud of being a Sheffielder.

Sheffield Forgemasters >

2010
Victor Mujakachi

Following the refusal of my asylum claim and the rejection of further evidence to re-open my case I became homeless and slept rough. I survive through the support of Assist Sheffield, a charity which helps destitute failed asylum seekers.

I feel at home in Sheffield. By volunteering with charities I gain a sense of belonging, but I miss my family and my country, Zimbabwe.

‹ SAFAR Charity Shop, Crookes

Paradise Square >

1968
Leni Solinger

I arrived in the UK from the USA just before May 1968, a very exciting time. Being left wing in America was a lonely thing; here there was so much happening. The anti-Vietnam war movement was huge. I became active in many campaigns and my union. Originally I planned to stay for a year. Almost 50 years later I am still here and still fighting for justice and equality, although the fight is getting harder and harder.

‹ Fir Vale Centre

1982
Abtisam Mohamed

My mother, sister and I came from the Yemen to join my father. He had been here since 1972 working in the steel industry with his father and uncles who had arrived 10 years earlier.

I'm now a solicitor and community activist, campaigning for the needs of disadvantaged areas and people. As a result of this work I was selected as an Olympic torchbearer in 2012.

1956

Josylin Allen

On arrival in Sheffield my friend and I were sent on a tramcar to Brightside, where we were asked to start working immediately. We looked for accommodation in Page Hall and Burngreave to no avail and were about to return to Birmingham when we finally found lodgings in Crookesmoor.

I settled in Sheffield and became the co-founder of the Sheffield and District Afro-Caribbean Association.

Crookesmoor Church >

Justine Brothwell

At the end of the second world war I was a young woman living in the city of Graz in Austria. Life was hard and food was short. The British Army was helping to feed schoolchildren and as my mother was a school caretaker we had close contact with the army cooks. One day a young man called Harold asked me to help him with the cooking - the beginning of our courtship. I went off skiing but he followed me so I knew he was serious! When I came back from skiing Harold got to know my parents better and once he'd had a few schnapps with my father everything was fine. But it was a further two years until we were married. The wedding was in Austria, Harold went back to Sheffield first and I was brought over to join him by the army in 1947.

‹ At home in Lowedges

1964

Haji Mohammad Nazir OBE

My father was a British Indian officer who fought for Britain in both world wars.

As part of the first influx to Sheffield from Pakistan, I was one of the few who spoke Punjabi, Urdu and English and spent many hours voluntarily interpreting. This led to a lifetime of service as an advice worker, a City Councillor and a member of forums such as Sheffield Campaign Against Racism.

‹ Madina Mosque

2009
Rodrigo Edema

Uganda has become a very hostile battleground to those in the opposition political group. I had no choice but to leave. I escaped persecution and survived the United Kingdom asylum system with resilience and good humour in my search for safety.

Now I work for City of Sanctuary Sheffield enabling asylum seekers and refugees to achieve their full potential and develop their skills towards independent living.

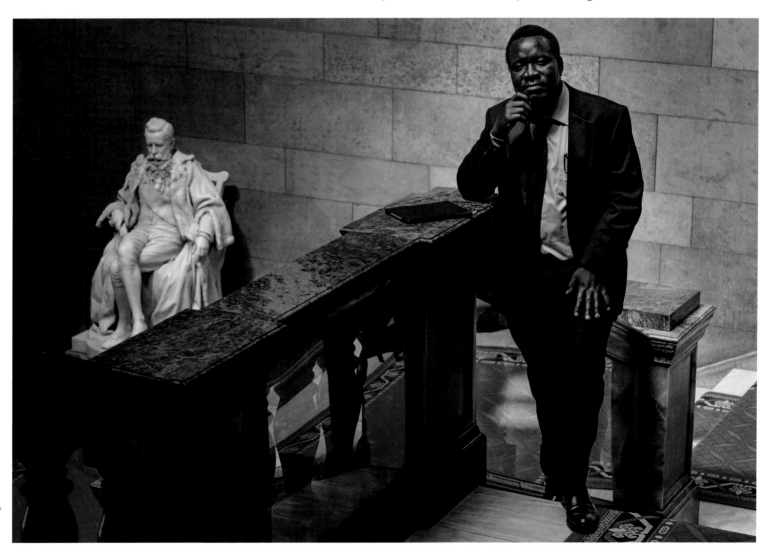

Sheffield Town Hall ›

Ana Maria Gonzalez

In 1973 a violent military coup took place in Chile. Thousands of people were tortured, others killed and more than 3,000 'disappeared'. Many members of my family were put in prison and tortured. In 1976 the repression was stronger than ever. My father, in home detention at the time, advised me to leave the country and I came to the UK. I could not travel back to Chile for 9 years, as I would risk being imprisoned. In the meantime my father died and I could not go to his funeral.

A fund from the World University Service enabled me to continue my studies at the University of London; I worked for many years at the University of Sheffield.

I have always felt very welcome in England and I have made it my second home. My son was born here and from only 5 years old he and I have supported Sheffield United together - true Blades. We still enjoy going to the matches together. When I visit Chile now it has changed so much that I consider myself a visitor or a tourist. While in Chile I long to come back to Sheffield to see my friends and son again.

‹ Bramall Lane

1997
Manuch

I was the director of a book publisher in Iran. We were not popular with the authorities; two of my partners were killed. We all would have have left the country but only I had the opportunity to do so. An offer to my wife from the University of Sheffield to do a Ph.D enabled us to escape.

I have two sons, both of whom are keen to be involved in British politics.

‹ Grave of Samuel Holberry,
Chartist leader, General Cemetery

2006

Magdalena Garpiel

My husband Adam and I left our successful business in Poland to learn another language and meet new people. Adam came first and got a job at The Druid's Inn in Birchover. I came six months later and we both worked at Thyme Cafe in Broomhill where Adam was Head Chef. Our daughter was born in 2012 and loves to go to Forge Dam to feed the ducks and hurtle down the slide.

Forge Dam Playground >

1985

Adam Yusuf

I initially came to the UK to study, but after two years the war in Somalia broke out. The situation was deteriorating and I couldn't return to my homeland and family. I chose to seek sanctuary and settle here.

Immigrants and refugees have contributed enormously positively to Sheffield, bringing new ideas and skills and enriching it's diversity. I have worked in public sector housing and the voluntary and private sectors.

‹ At home in Shirecliffe

1978

Araya
Redda

In my youth I was presented with an award by Emperor Haile Selassie. But the country was ready for change and I was part of the peasant and student uprising that deposed the Emperor, only to be replaced by a ruthless military junta that terrorised the nation through mass inquisitions, murder, arrest or forced exile. My exit through a scholarship for postgraduate studies was one of the lucky ones. Sheffield welcomed me and gave me respite from a nightmare.

At home in Nether Edge >

1981

Cher Kheng Lee

I came to Yorkshire from Malaysia to complete my education. Arriving in Sheffield as a graduate for my first job, I commuted to and from Castleton daily by coach. It was an exciting time, a big adventure.

One rainy November night in 1985, I met a visiting pen friend at the coach station. From the moment Ian stepped off that coach from Newcastle, we knew that we would be together. Little did we know then it would be for a very happy 27 years. We had our civil partnership in 2008 but I lost Ian to cancer in 2013.

Time marches on, I have worked at Sheffield Hallam University since 1986. Sheffield coach station is now Sheffield Interchange. Sheffield city remains my home, where my heart and happy memories reside.

I am waiting for my coach, my next big adventure.

1989
Patrick Meleady

My Irish grandfather had been a British soldier. This was vital for my family's sense of belonging when we came to the UK and experienced racism in the days of 'No Black's, No Dogs and No Irish'.

I discovered Sheffield when my sisters were involved in the miners' and steel workers' strikes.

My wife is from Bangladesh; our families hold strong Yorkshire values but also have unique ethnicities and traditions that are part of the cultural tapestry that makes Britain so Great.

‹ Pitsmoor Adventure Playground

Millennium Gallery >

1972

Dipti Aistrop

When Asian families were evicted from Uganda by Idi Amin my family were granted asylum in the UK. I remember the kindness of WRVS volunteers who befriended new arrivals, provided warm clothing and invited me to their Christmas celebration!

I studied nursing before moving to Sheffield with my husband. Sheffield is a wonderful city where my children have grown up and I feel proud to be part of it.

Aroose Uppal

When I was a child in Uganda my family lived a comfortable life. Until Idi Amin came to power. All Ugandan Asians were given three months to leave the country. We left on the last plane to Pakistan and became stateless as we did not have passports. A year later my grandmother, who lived in the UK, became ill and my father tried to bring us to the UK. We travelled through Afghanistan, Iran, Iraq, Turkey, Yugoslavia, Bulgaria and finally Austria, where we were accepted as refugees. We lived in a refugee camp for two years. My father applied to live in England but was rejected; Sweden agreed to take us.

As the first migrants to the small town of Trollhättan virtually everything we did made the local newspaper! I started formal education aged 11, progressing to university. Every summer we came to England to visit family and I eventually settled here.

My experiences led me into working to help others. I started as an advice and advocacy worker for the Asian Welfare Association and for the last twenty years I have worked for St. Mary's Church and Community Centre. I can't leave Sheffield, it's always been good to me.

‹ St. Mary's Church and Community Centre

1970

Rukhsar
Khan

When I was seven we came to England from Pakistan to join my father who was working in Sheffield's steel works.

When studying for my A-Levels, I attended a conference at Firth Hall chaired by David Blunkett. I asserted that "unless the Labour Party were to adjust their policies towards the centre right they would be unelectable". I was vindicated when Tony Blair did exactly that. I went on to read Law at the London School of Economics.

‹ Firth Hall, University of Sheffield

Machon Bank Road >

1967

Claudette McKoy

I arrived in Sheffield on a grey, damp day. It was scary to leave the only family I had ever known to join parents I had no memory of and siblings I had never met. I was two when my father left to work in the UK and three when my mother left me with my grandmother to join him.

Coming from sunny Jamaica I found Sheffield ugly but I have learnt to appreciate its beauty.

Isilda Lang

I arrived in Sheffield on a misty, grey, damp April day in 1977. It was a very scary time for me leaving Chile, the only place I had ever known. As a refugee escaping political persecution it was terrible to suffer torture, fear and nightmares of persecution. Being displaced from the place you were born is not easy, because you have to readjust to everything, to practically be reborn. The language was the hardest thing to learn - it took me five years to have the confidence to speak English.

I've become involved in the communities I've lived in. I started helping in the playgroup my son attended. Later, with a group of friends, we set up the St James' Parent and Toddler group in Pitsmoor and I'm still play leader there.

In 1982 I joined the Red Cross, becoming a Nursing Welfare officer, teaching children and adults first aid. I was part of the Red Cross when another tragedy happened in my life, the Hillsborough disaster of April 1989, where I worked alongside doctors and nurses on the day.

Roe Wood >

2008
Mamen Vicente

My wanderlust took me from Alicante to Ibiza in 1999, but I wanted to improve my English and a friend recommended Edinburgh.

When I first came to Sheffield to visit my partner I was still living in Edinburgh. I was immediately drawn to Sheffield and was well aware of its vibrant musical heritage as much of my youth was spent listening to its bands. I now consider it my home.

< Endcliffe Park

1955

Jean
Bentley

I was the sixth of eleven children. Dad had a smallholding that produced all the fruits and foods grown in Jamaica.

When I came to England I was accepted for nurse training, eventually becoming a midwife, then a health visitor. I married a Yorkshireman; we came to Sheffield with our son and my husband worked at the Polytechnic.

My allotment is a place to escape and find peace; it reminds me of my childhood.

Highcliffe Allotments ›

‹ Manor Oaks Farm

2002

Renata Gargala

I grew up during the Communist era, when travel outside Poland was not permitted. When I was 16 the Berlin Wall fell and I felt as if the world was opening up. I travelled throughout Europe and met my English future husband who was travelling overland by bicycle.

As a child I loved the time I spent in the Polish countryside. Sheffield enables me to visit the Peak District with my family and friends; this is what I love most about living here.

1961
Ghulam Nabi

Following the partition of Pakistan from India there were few jobs in Azad Kashmir. The UK needed labour from Commonwealth countries so I came to Sheffield to find a better life. As more families arrived a thriving Kashmiri Muslim community was established.

Many people lived in poor housing. I was involved in starting Darnall Housing Co-op, which provided high quality housing for forty families. Now Kashmir Gardens is a community of families of Kashmiri, English and Somali origin, all living together in a peaceful environment.

Kashmir Gardens, Darnall ›

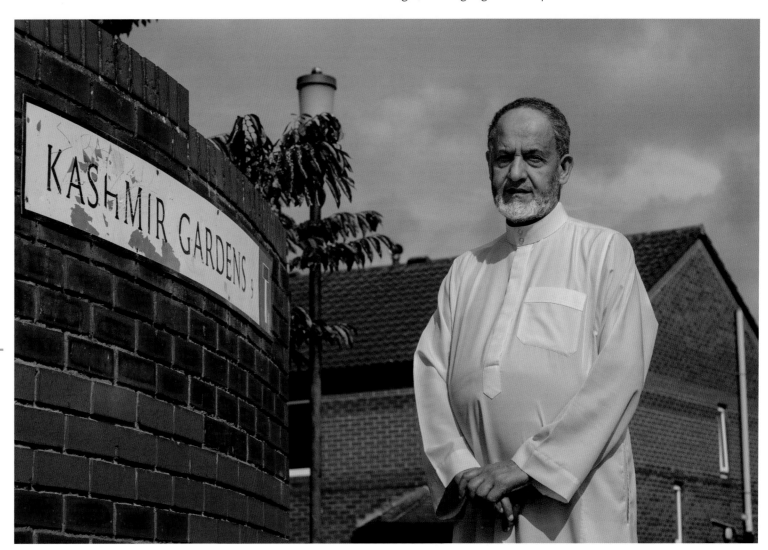

Abdi Aziz Suleiman

I came to Sheffield with my mother, having been born in Somalia during the civil war 3 years earlier. I loved Broomhall but growing up was a daily challenge. Every road sign, instruction manual and bureaucratic letter was another mystery for us to solve as a team. We did homework together as we both needed to know what it was that the British called a tufaax (apple); or how to share amazement at the occasional Hilaac iyo onkod (lightning and thunder). We even put up with the casual racism that came our way together. I guess we thought it was to be expected, though I slowly began to realise that racism, no matter how casual, was like a grenade thrown at the foundations of your carefully constructed confidence. I went on to study at the University of Sheffield, become President of the Students' Union in Sheffield , now work at the University of Sheffield and become a school governor at my old secondary school (Silverdale). So you'd be correct to say much of who I am is the product of this city.

‹ Broomhall flats

2005

Habib
Josefi

The day I was told that I could come and live in England was the happiest of my life. I would no longer be forced to move from country to country in search of sanctuary.

My family had been forced to flee from Afghanistan to Iran three times as regimes changed and foreigners intervened in the country. When the Taliban took over, I was forced to flee yet again. I was a teenager at the time and had no formal education.

I moved around the world trying to find a permanent home, spending time in Iran, Turkey and Russia before finding temporary sanctuary in Cuba. I was halfway through my first year at University when I was told I must find somewhere else to go and the UK accepted me as a refugee. I had to learn English almost from scratch. I wanted to understand this society and to make it my home.

Utilising the Spanish I had learned in Cuba, I studied for a degree in Hispanic Studies and graduated from the University of Sheffield in 2010 and subsequently developed a career as an interpreter in Spanish, Farsi and Dari.

Weston Park ›

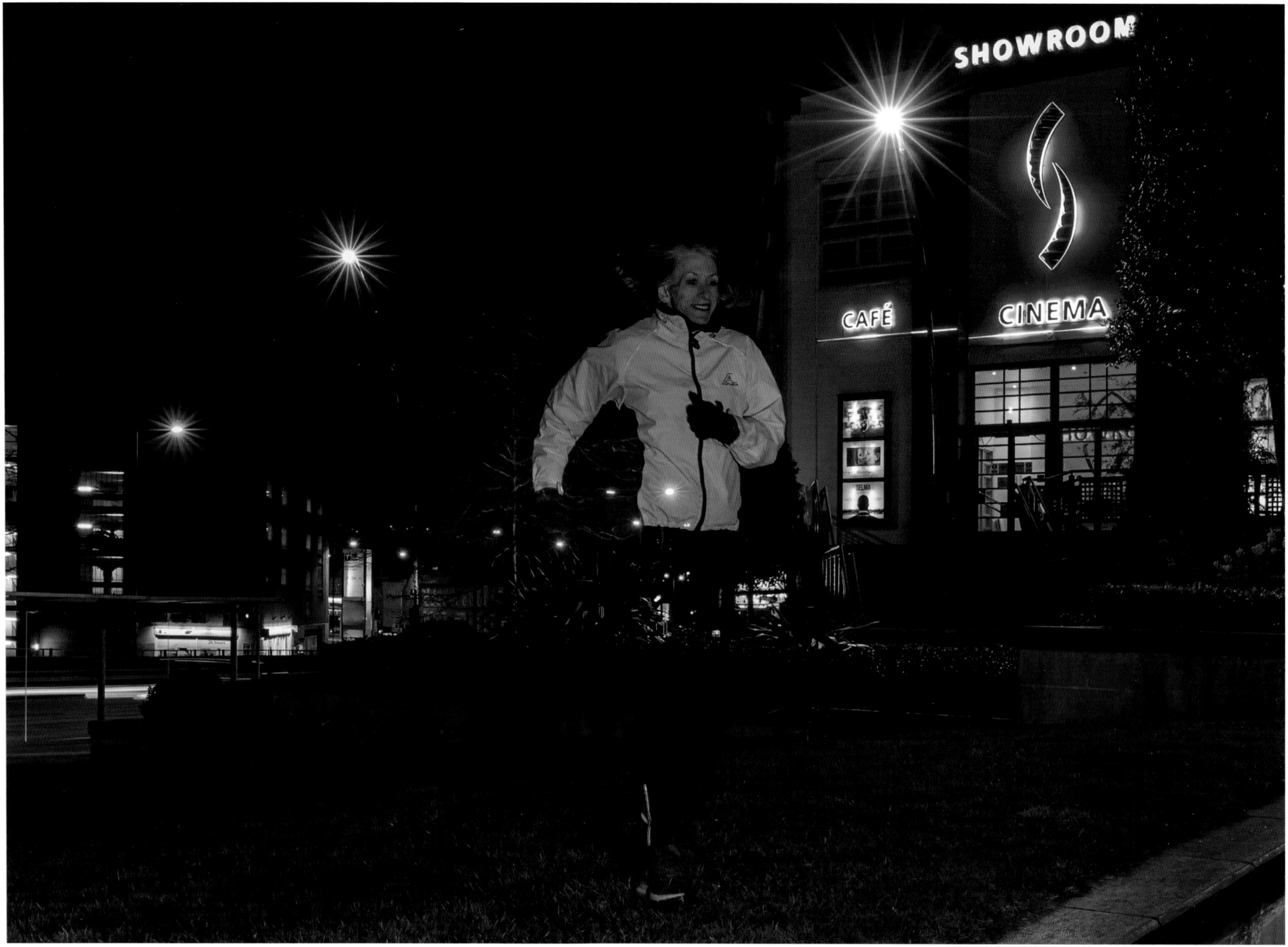
SHOWROOM
CAFÉ
CINEMA

2001

Liz Crowther

Reading books by English writers was an inherent part of my Australian childhood. I adored the tiny books and illustrations of Beatrice Potter and devoured books about ponies and boarding schools. Each month my mother bought me 'June And School Friend' and I silently slipped into England.

My family had evolved from a mixture of English, Irish, Scottish and Finnish culture, so I had been brought up on a hybrid of traditions and beliefs. Not only did we listen to and watch British radio and TV programmes, including The Bill, but we stood to God Save The Queen at the cinema. And at Christmas we gave cards with snow scenes even though it was blisteringly hot!

In my teenage years Jane Eyre and Lorna Doone, along with my brother's Beatles, Rolling Stones and Van Morrison records, must have been subliminal messages, leading me to the UK! So when I had the opportunity to experience the real thing in 2001 as a teacher of English, I knew it would be a life changing experience. I remember driving to school in 2001, thinking, 'Wow! I am in Sheffield, England! How amazing is that?'

2014

Rawan Dardok
& Ahmed Maani

Ahmed and I met at University in Nablus. He then studied for a Master's degree at Edinburgh University, and when he was offered a job in Sheffield he asked me to join him. It was a hard decision, as it meant leaving my lonely mother and my ill brother in Palestine, where going home safe is all that people wish for.

Sheffield is warm, welcoming, and accepting. We are happy and grateful for our new hopeful life.

‹ Sheffield Cathedral

Christet Church Stannington >

1996

Danny Piermattei

Little did I know as a teenager growing up in Italy that a summer job as a barman would lead to Sheffield, the home of the girl I was to marry.

After twenty years in Stannington I am proud to call this green and hilly part of Yorkshire my home. My voluntary work helping to preserve the environment gives me strong ties to a place where I have always been made welcome.

Maria Olschefsky

The 'Blue Danube' scheme to recruit girls to work in British factories was a big adventure for me. After the war there was nothing but cleaning jobs in the tiny Austrian village of Ebental. So I signed up to come to Britain enthusiastically, although my Austrian mother and Russian father were not best pleased. The Ministry of Labour insisted we were unattached, not pregnant and in perfect health - we were very thoroughly examined!

We were given lovely accommodation when we arrived. Although I was Austrian and could speak English, some people thought I was German and called me a 'Nazi'. But many people were kind and invited me in for tea.

We were only allowed to stay for two years and had to work in the cotton mills. The noise of 50 looms working was horrendous, but the money was good and we had a great time in the pubs and dance halls. I started courting - he was a double bass player in a jazz band and when we were married it meant I could stay permanently. We moved to Sheffield together and I've been here for nearly 60 years.

At home in Burngreave >

< Pakistan Muslim Centre, Attercliffe

1958

Mohammed Younis

My grandfather came before World War Two, my father came in 1952. I arrived from Pakistan as an 11 year old and only attended secondary school for three years. I first trained as a skilled machinist in the engineering industry, then joined the council's Youth Service and achieved an MA in International Politics and Security Studies. In the late 1980s I helped to found the Pakistan Muslim Centre.

2007

Ales Pokuta &
Maria Pokutova

Racism is worse in Slovakia than in England, so it's hard for Roma people to find work and provide for their children. I came here with my family from the small village of Žehra. We couldn't speak English when we first arrived and that made it hard to find jobs. Maria came here in 2013; we met here.

Now I speak English and I want my children to adopt English culture.

At home in Pitsmoor ›

< West Don Street

1966

Lynn
Bent

I was 15 when my mother, brother, sister and I left Jamaica to join my father who had been here since 1962. I worked for a cutlery firm for three years whilst studying English and Maths. I then worked as an Auxiliary Nurse at Nether Edge Hospital, moving to Weston Park Hospital until retirement.

I became involved in the West Indian Association as a committee councillor and member of the women's group.

1980
Danielle Barbereau

Born in France, I studied English and Interpreting at the University of Angers. Living here was a life-long dream fuelled by avid readings of Jane Eyre. Now, as a keen hillwalker, I can explore Bronte country in Yorkshire and Derbyshire.

What initially struck me about Sheffield, apart from the steeps hills, was the amount of green spaces, trees and how friendly the people were. I enjoy living near Sharrowvale Road and its quirky shops and village atmosphere.

Starmore Boss wine merchant, Sharrow Vale ›

1984

Zameer Khan

My family lived in rural Kashmir. A beautiful place, but little work. There was a shortage of labour in the UK so Pakistanis were invited to come to the UK. Big strapping guys from rural Kashmir were thought to be particularly suitable for heavy manual labour jobs such as the steel mills! So my father came in 1968 and worked for a steel plating company in Slough. In 1984 I came to join him with my mother and three siblings. After a week in Slough I was packed off to visit an aunty in Sheffield. I liked Sheffield, because it was green and hilly like Kashmir. So I stayed and went to school here and a year later the rest of the family joined me.

School wasn't wholly successful for me because of language barriers, but at college I studied leisure and tourism and motor vehicle engineering. Now I drive a taxi and work voluntarily as a football coach, for the One Nation gym and at the Madina Mosque.

‹ U-Mix Centre

Angga Kara

In 1997 I left Bandung in Indonesia for Sheffield. My Dad was doing a PhD at the University of Sheffield. It was also my Mum's dream to live in England and take me and my siblings as well to broaden our horizons. All I remember is being told we were going, next thing I was freezing at Gatwick airport wearing shorts!

I soon settled in and the people of Sheffield embraced me and changed me to the person I am today. I've met people from all over the world and many have inspired me to believe that anything is possible as long as I put my mind to it. I like to do the same for others now through my work as a fashion designer, social entrepreneur and dancer.

Sheffield has a great sense of community and belonging. Home is where the heart is and mine is here now. I have an English wife and we have a great life here together with our amazing friends and family.

In my opinion, there is no place like the north.
No other place like Sheffield.
No place like home.
Let's hope for a brighter future ahead.

South Street Park >

Acknowledgements

To make a good portrait the subject must give generously, not only of their time, but of themselves. I am fortunate that so many people were willing to work with me and give something of themselves and I am enormously grateful to them all.

I am equally grateful to everyone who helped me to find the people you see in this book; finding people can take much, much longer than taking pictures.

I also want to thank the following people for their generous financial support of this book:

Alison Abrahams
Daniel Abrahams
Danielle Barbereau
Phil and Penny Borkett
Peter Butler
May and Neville Chipulina
Liz Clough
Roy Cuckow
Penny Dembo and Andy Rixham
Laurence and Michel Fisbein
Mike Fitter

Linda Green
Simon Green
Majella Kilkey
David and Gillian Lister
Reina Lister
Dora Meredith
Karen and Tom Nuttgens
Northend Creative Print Solutions
Danny Piermattei
Hannah Saxelby-Newall
Seb Schmoller
Seven Hills Bakery
Jane and Michael Thomas
Rachel Walker
Sylvia Ward
Jan Watson
Ken Woodhouse

Finally, I would like to thank my wife, Linda, and my children Alison and Daniel, for their unstinting and unending encouragement, support and critical friendship throughout the three years it took to complete this project.